Brevard ABCs

Learning Your ABCs By Looking Around You

Alex Schierholtz

Full Court Press
Englewood Cliffs, New Jersey

First Edition

Copyright © 2025 by Alex Schierholtz

All rights reserved. No part of this book may be
reproduced or transmitted in any form or by any means electronic
or mechanical, including by photocopying,
by recording, or by any information storage and retrieval system,
without the express permission of the author,
except where permitted by law.

Published in the United States of America
by Full Court Press, 601 Palisade Avenue,
Englewood Cliffs, NJ 07632
fullcourtpress.com

TO MY DAUGHTER KINSLEY
You are my why, always and forever.
"Give Kinsley hugs and kisses for me"—Grandma Lisa.

All art and text by the author.

ISBN 978-1-953728-49-4
Library of Congress Control No. 2025917725

Book design by Barry Sheinkopf

A : Artemis

The Artemis rocket is NASA's biggest and most powerful rocket. It's designed to take astronauts to the Moon and help prepare for future missions to Mars.

B : Bridge

The A. Max Brewer Bridge in Titusville crosses the Indian River with wide views of the water. It leads to the Merritt Island Wildlife Refuge and Kennedy Space Center.

C : Cocoa Beach Pier

The Cocoa Beach Pier stretches 800 feet over the ocean. Visitors come to fish, eat, shop, and enjoy the sea breeze.

D : Da Kine

Da Kine Diego's in Satellite Beach is a relaxed, surf-themed spot known for fresh fish tacos and Hawaiian-style dishes.

E : Erna Nixon Park

Erna Nixon Park in Melbourne has a winding boardwalk through shady Florida forest. It's a peaceful place to walk and spot wildlife.

F : Fireworks

At Dragon Point, fireworks light up the night sky over the Indian and Banana Rivers, drawing crowds to watch the colorful display.

G : Galaxy Skateway

Galaxy Skateway in Melbourne is a classic roller skating rink with music, lights, and open skate times for all ages.

H : Harvey's

Harvey's Groves was a longtime local favorite for fresh oranges and juice. Though it's closed now, it's still fondly remembered.

I : Indian River Lagoon

The Indian River Lagoon is full of wildlife, from dolphins and manatees to hundreds of bird and fish species. It's a favorite place for boating, fishing, and kayaking.

J : Jetty Park

Jetty Park in Cape Canaveral has a beach, a fishing pier, and a great view for watching cruise ships and rocket launches.

K : Kelly Slater

The Kelly Slater statue in Cocoa Beach honors the world champion surfer who grew up here.

L : Long Doggers

Long Doggers is a local restaurant known for seafood, tropical drinks, and a laid-back atmosphere.

M : Mathers Bridge

Mathers Bridge is a historic drawbridge that connects Merritt Island to Indian Harbour Beach, offering pretty views of the water.

N : NASA

The Vehicle Assembly Building at Kennedy Space Center is one of the largest buildings in the world. It's where rockets are stacked before launch.

O : Ocean

Pelican Beach Park in Satellite Beach is a family-friendly spot with sandy shores, picnic areas, and ocean views.

P : Patrick Space Force Base

Patrick Space Force Base supports rocket launches, satellite tracking, and national defense.

Q : Quiet Flight

Quiet Flight Surfboards makes quality boards for surfers looking for top performance on the waves.

R : Ron Jon

Ron Jon Surf Shop in Cocoa Beach is open 24 hours and sells surfboards, beachwear, and gear for all things coastal.

S : Sebastian Inlet

Sebastian Inlet is a top spot for fishing, surfing, and seeing ocean wildlife.

T : Turkey Creek

Turkey Creek Sanctuary in Palm Bay has boardwalks and trails through wetlands, perfect for hiking and birdwatching.

U : University

Florida Institute of Technology in Melbourne is a university focused on science, engineering, and technology.

V : Villon

Villon's Coffee in Satellite Beach and Melbourne is known for fresh-brewed coffee and a welcoming atmosphere.

W : Wetlands

Viera Wetlands has walking trails, observation areas, and plenty of birds and wildlife to see.

X : SpaceX

SpaceX builds reusable rockets and spacecraft, working toward missions to Mars and beyond.

Y : Yacht Club

Melbourne Yacht Club is a place for sailing, dining, and community events along the Indian River Lagoon.

Z : Zoo

Brevard Zoo has animals, kayak rides, and hands-on activities that teach about nature and conservation.

www.ingramcontent.com/pod-product-compliance
Lightning Source LLC
LaVergne TN
LVHW072127070426
835512LV00002B/36